HOW TO DEAL WITH ANXIETY

How to stop overthinking and unnecessary worrying about things

Michelle Brahms

TABLE OF CONTENT

INTRODUCTION

Everyone experiences anxiety from time to time—it's a normal part of life. But what if your anxiety persists and won't go away despite your best efforts to brush it off? This is where you need more than just a mental reset: you need therapeutic care to support your mental health.

Consider the words of Sonia, a patient with Generalized Anxiety Disorder (GAD), who said, "Sometimes my head feels heavy because I think and worry about multiple things at a time." Many people can relate to this feeling of excessive worry and fear about events that haven't happened or may never happen.

It's a common misconception that you can simply flip away anxious thoughts or that anxiety is just a byproduct of stress. These are myths. Persistent and excessive anxiety often requires professional intervention because it can lead to severe consequences if left untreated.

To avoid such outcomes, recognizing the need for mental health treatment is crucial. Accepting yourself as someone who may need professional help is the first step toward managing and reducing your anxiety.

So, how can you help yourself? This book provides all the guidance you need to understand anxiety, identify when it requires urgent attention, and discover practical methods to manage or overcome it. You'll find comprehensive strategies and insights to retrain your mind towards a healthier lifestyle. With this book, you won't need another resource; it offers everything you need to tackle anxiety effectively.

CHAPTER 1
Understanding Anxiety

Finally we are here in the beginning of our journey to understand and manage anxiety. Let's start by breaking down what anxiety really is. At its core, anxiety is your body's natural response to stress. It's a feeling of fear or apprehension about what's to come. For example, you might feel anxious on the first day of school, going to a job interview, or giving a speech. This kind of anxiety is normal and often useful. It can help you stay alert and focused, push you to action, and motivate you to solve problems.

However, anxiety can become overwhelming, making it hard to cope with daily life. When these feelings are constant and intense, you might be dealing with an anxiety disorder. There are several types of anxiety disorders, including:

Generalized Anxiety Disorder (GAD): This involves excessive, unrealistic worry and tension, even if there's little or nothing to provoke the anxiety.

Panic Disorder: You experience sudden, intense fear that brings on a panic attack. During these attacks, you may sweat, have chest pain, and feel palpitations (unusually strong or irregular heartbeats). Sometimes you may feel like you're choking or having a heart attack.

Social Anxiety Disorder: This involves overwhelming worry and self-consciousness about everyday social situations. You obsessively worry about others judging you or being embarrassed.

Specific Phobias: This is an intense fear of a specific object or situation, like heights, flying, or spiders. The fear goes beyond what's appropriate and may cause you to avoid ordinary situations.

Common Symptoms and Triggers

Recognizing the signs of anxiety is the first step toward managing it. Symptoms can be physical, emotional, and behavioral. You might experience:

Physical Symptoms: Increased heart rate, sweating, trembling, feeling weak or tired, trouble sleeping, gastrointestinal (GI) problems.

Emotional Symptoms: Feelings of impending doom, panic, or nervousness.

Behavioral Symptoms: Avoiding places or situations to prevent anxiety, becoming overly cautious.

Triggers are things that can cause your anxiety to flare up. They vary from person to person but often include:

Stress at Work: Tight deadlines, high expectations, and office conflicts.

School Pressures: Exams, peer pressure, and high academic standards.

Financial Concerns: Debt, unexpected expenses, or job instability.

Health Issues: Chronic illness, a bad diagnosis, or concern about a loved one's health.

Relationship Problems: Conflict with partners, friends, or family members.

The Science Behind Anxiety: Brain and Body Connections

Understanding how anxiety works in your body can make it feel less mysterious and more manageable. When you face a perceived threat, your brain's alarm system, called the amygdala, kicks into high gear. It sends a distress signal to another part of your brain called the hypothalamus. This sets off a chain reaction in your body, releasing stress hormones like adrenaline and cortisol. These hormones prepare your body to either fight or flee the threat.

This response is helpful in dangerous situations but less so in your everyday life. If you're constantly anxious, your body stays in this heightened state, which can be exhausting and harmful over time.

Myths and Misconceptions about Anxiety

There are many myths about anxiety that can prevent people from seeking help or understanding their experiences. Let's clear up a few:

Myth 1: Anxiety is just stress: While stress can contribute to anxiety, they are not the same. Stress is a response to a threat in a situation, while anxiety is a reaction to the stress.

Myth 2: Anxiety isn't a real illness: Anxiety disorders are genuine, serious medical conditions that require treatment, just like diabetes or hypertension.

Myth 3: You can just snap out of it: Managing anxiety often requires more than just willpower. It can involve therapy, medication, lifestyle changes, and learning new coping skills.

Myth 4: Only weak people get anxiety: Anxiety can affect anyone, regardless of strength, background, or personality.

When you know what anxiety is, recognizing its symptoms and triggers, learning how it affects your brain and body, and dispelling common myths, you're already taking significant steps toward managing it. Remember, knowledge is power, and understanding anxiety is the first step to overcoming it. In the following chapters, we'll dive deeper into strategies and techniques to help you handle anxiety effectively. Together, we can navigate the path to a calmer, more peaceful life.

CHAPTER 2
Identifying Your Anxiety Triggers

Anxiety can feel like a shadow, always lurking nearby, but understanding what triggers it can help you take control. In this chapter, we'll explore how to identify your anxiety triggers and develop strategies to manage them. Come let get a tour together

Recognizing Personal Triggers

Recognizing what triggers your anxiety is the first step toward managing it. Everyone's triggers are different, and what might cause anxiety for one person might not affect another at all. Here's how you can start identifying yours:

Reflect on Recent Experiences: Think about the last few times you felt anxious. What were you doing? Who were you with? What thoughts were running through your mind?

Note Physical Reactions: Pay attention to how your body reacts. Do your palms sweat, does your heart race, or do you feel a knot in your stomach? These physical signs can help pinpoint what sets off your anxiety.

Emotional Responses: Notice your emotions. Are there certain feelings, like fear or sadness that often accompany your anxiety? Understanding these can provide clues to your triggers.

Taking time to reflect on these aspects helps you get closer to identifying your specific triggers.

Keeping an Anxiety Journal

An anxiety journal is a powerful tool for tracking your triggers. By writing down your experiences, you can identify patterns and gain insights into what causes your anxiety.

Daily Entries: Each day, write about your feelings and experiences. Note any moments of anxiety, what was happening at the time, and how you felt physically and emotionally.

Patterns and Trends: After a few weeks, review your entries. Look for common themes or situations that repeatedly appear before or during your anxiety episodes.

Specifics Matter: Be as detailed as possible. Mention the time of day, the location, the people involved, and your specific thoughts and feelings.

Keeping an anxiety journal requires commitment, but it can provide invaluable insights into your anxiety patterns.

Patterns and Trends in Anxiety Episodes

Understanding patterns in your anxiety can make it more manageable. By recognizing these trends, you can anticipate and prepare for situations that might trigger anxiety.

Time and Place: Notice if your anxiety spikes at certain times of the day or in specific locations. For example, do you feel more anxious in the morning before work, or does it peak when you're in crowded places?

Social Contexts: Are there certain people or types of social interactions that heighten your anxiety? Identifying these can help you develop strategies to cope or avoid triggering situations when possible.

Activities and Tasks: Pay attention to tasks or activities that make you anxious. It could be something like public speaking, meeting deadlines, or even everyday chores.

Recognizing these patterns empowers you to make changes in your routine and environment to reduce anxiety triggers.

Strategies for Managing Triggers

Once you've identified your triggers, the next step is to develop strategies to manage them. Here are some practical steps you can take:

Prepare and Plan: If you know certain situations trigger your anxiety, prepare for them in advance. For instance, if public speaking makes you anxious, practice your speech multiple times and visualize a successful presentation.

Relaxation Techniques: Incorporate relaxation techniques into your daily routine. Deep breathing, progressive muscle relaxation, and mindfulness can help calm your mind and body before anxiety sets in.

Positive Affirmations: Use positive affirmations to challenge negative thoughts that fuel your anxiety. Replace thoughts like "I can't handle this" with "I am capable and strong."

Seek Support: Don't hesitate to seek support from friends, family, or a therapist. Sometimes talking about your anxiety and getting a different perspective can make a big difference.

By taking proactive steps and using these strategies, you can better manage your anxiety triggers and reduce their impact on your life.

Remember, you are not alone in this journey, and with patience and persistence, you can gain control over your anxiety. Stay kind to yourself, and take each step one day at a time.

CHAPTER 3
Mindfulness and Meditation Techniques

Anxiety can feel overwhelming, but mindfulness and meditation can be powerful tools to help you regain control and find peace. This chapter will guide you through practical techniques and exercises that you can easily incorporate into your daily life.

Introduction to Mindfulness

Mindfulness is all about being present in the moment. It means paying attention to what you're experiencing right now without judging it. When you're mindful, you're fully aware of your thoughts, feelings, and surroundings, which can help reduce anxiety.

Imagine sitting quietly, just focusing on your breath. Feel the air coming in and going out. This simple act of paying attention to your breathing can help calm your mind. You're not trying to change anything; you're just noticing it. This is the essence of mindfulness.

Guided Meditation Practices

Meditation is a practice that helps you develop mindfulness. There are many types of meditation, but they all involve focusing your mind and eliminating distractions. Here are a few types you can try:

1. Body Scan Meditation

- Find a comfortable place to sit or lie down.
- Close your eyes and take a few deep breaths.
- Start by focusing on your toes. Notice any sensations without trying to change them.
- Gradually move your attention up your body, part by part, until you reach the top of your head.

2. Loving-Kindness Meditation

- Sit comfortably and close your eyes.
- Take a few deep breaths.
- Imagine sending love and kindness to yourself. Repeat phrases like, "May I be happy. May I be healthy."
- Gradually extend these wishes to others: first to loved ones, then to acquaintances, and even to people you find difficult.

3. Mindful Breathing

- Sit in a comfortable position and close your eyes.

- Focus on your breathing. Feel the air entering your nose, filling your lungs, and then leaving your body.
- If your mind wanders, gently bring it back to your breath.

Breathing Exercises for Immediate Relief

When you feel anxious, your breathing often becomes shallow and rapid. Practicing deep breathing can help calm your nervous system. Here are a few exercises to try:

1. **4-7-8 Breathing**

- Inhale through your nose for 4 seconds.
- Hold your breath for 7 seconds.
- Exhale through your mouth for 8 seconds.
- Repeat this cycle a few times.

2. **Box Breathing**

- Inhale for 4 seconds.
- Hold your breath for 4 seconds.
- Exhale for 4 seconds.
- Hold your breath for 4 seconds.
- Continue this pattern for a few minutes.

3. **Abdominal Breathing**

- Place one hand on your chest and the other on your abdomen.
- Take a deep breath in through your nose, allowing your abdomen to rise.
- Exhale slowly through your mouth.
- Focus on making your abdomen, not your chest, rise and fall with each breath.

Incorporating Mindfulness into Daily Life

Mindfulness isn't just for meditation sessions; it's a way of living. Here are some ways to bring mindfulness into your everyday activities:

1. **Mindful Eating**

- Take time to notice the colors, smells, and textures of your food.
- Eat slowly, savoring each bite.
- Pay attention to the flavors and how your body feels as you eat.

2. **Mindful Walking**

- As you walk, notice how your feet feel when they touch the ground.
- Pay attention to your surroundings—the sights, sounds, and smells.

- Try to walk without rushing, focusing on the experience of walking itself.

3. **Mindful Listening**

- When someone is speaking to you, give them your full attention.
- Listen to the words, tone, and emotions they are expressing.
- Avoid interrupting and let them finish before you respond.

Practicing mindfulness can help you feel more grounded and less overwhelmed by anxiety. Start with small steps, and gradually, it will become a natural part of your daily life. Remember, the goal isn't to eliminate anxiety completely, but to manage it in a way that it doesn't control you. Take it one moment at a time, and be kind to yourself on this journey.

CHAPTER 4
Cognitive-Behavioral Strategies

Welcome to Chapter 4. Here, we'll explore practical strategies you can use to manage your anxiety. This isn't just about learning techniques; it's about finding ways to change how you think and feel, making your journey with anxiety a bit easier to navigate. Come with me and discover these cognitive-behavioral strategies.

Understanding Cognitive-Behavioral Therapy (CBT)

Cognitive-Behavioral Therapy, or CBT, is a type of talk therapy that helps you understand how your thoughts, feelings, and behaviors are interconnected. Think of it as a way to rewire your brain to react differently to stressors.

What is CBT?

CBT is about recognizing and challenging the thoughts that cause anxiety. It's like having a toolkit for your mind, helping you tackle negative thinking patterns and replace them with more positive ones.

How Does CBT Work?

CBT works by breaking down your problems into smaller parts and addressing each one. It helps you focus on the present moment and develop practical skills to deal with your issues right now, rather than dwelling on the past or worrying about the future.

Identifying and Challenging Negative Thoughts

Negative thoughts can be sneaky and powerful, often driving our anxiety without us even realizing it. These are ways to to spot these thoughts and what to do about them.

Spotting Negative Thoughts

Start by paying attention to your inner dialogue. When you feel anxious, ask yourself what thoughts are going through your mind. Write them down if it helps. This can make it easier to see patterns and identify which thoughts are triggering your anxiety.

Challenging These Thoughts

Once you've identified a negative thought, it's time to challenge it. Ask yourself:

- Is this thought based on facts or feelings?

- What evidence do I have that supports or contradicts this thought?
- Is there another way to look at this situation?

By questioning the validity of your negative thoughts, you can start to weaken their hold on you.

Developing Healthy Thought Patterns

Now that you know how to challenge negative thoughts, let's work on building healthier ones.

Positive Affirmations

Use positive affirmations to replace negative thoughts. For example, if you find yourself thinking, "I can't handle this," counter it with, "I've faced challenges before and managed them."

Reframing

Reframing is about looking at a situation from a different perspective. Instead of seeing a mistake as a failure, view it as a learning opportunity. This shift in perspective can reduce anxiety and build resilience.

Practical CBT Exercises for Anxiety Management

Let's get hands-on with some CBT exercises that you can practice daily.

Thought Records

A thought record is a tool to track your negative thoughts, the situations that trigger them, and how you respond. This can help you see patterns and work on changing them.

Behavioral Experiments

Test out your negative thoughts by conducting small experiments. For instance, if you're anxious about social situations, plan a small social outing and observe what happens. Often, the outcome is not as scary as our thoughts make it out to be.

Exposure Therapy

Gradually exposing yourself to the things that cause you anxiety can help reduce your fear over time. Start with small, manageable steps and gradually work your way up to more challenging situations.

Final Thoughts

Remember, using cognitive-behavioral strategies takes practice and patience. You won't see changes overnight, but with consistent effort, you can retrain your brain to handle anxiety in a healthier way. Keep a positive outlook, and know that each step you take brings you closer to a more peaceful state of mind. You're not alone in this journey— many have walked this path before and found their way to a better place, and you can too. Keep going, and be kind to yourself along the way.

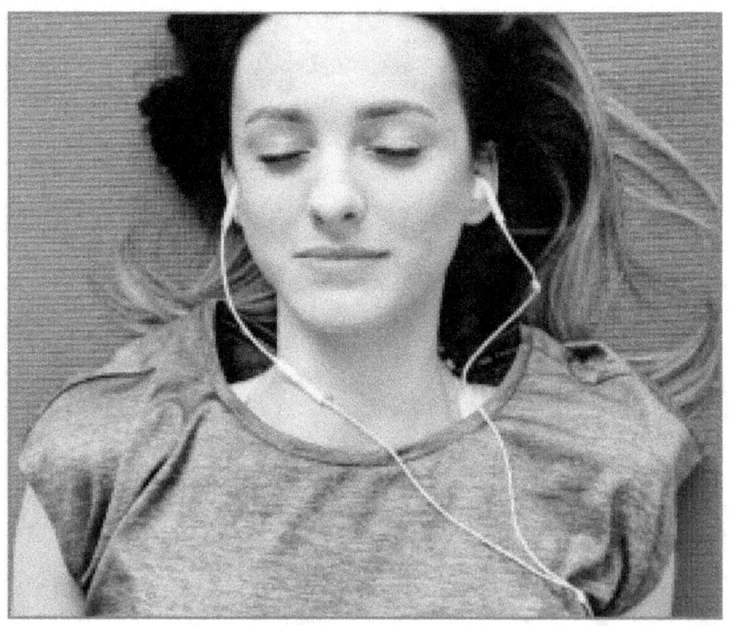

CHAPTER 5
Lifestyle Changes for Anxiety Reduction

Welcome to Chapter 5! In this chapter, we'll explore how making simple changes to your lifestyle can help you manage and reduce anxiety. Let's walk through some practical tips together, so you can start feeling more in control and at ease.

The Role of Diet and Nutrition

Eating for a Calm Mind

What you eat can have a big impact on how you feel. It's not just about physical health; your diet affects your mental health too. Here are some tips to help you eat in a way that supports a calm and balanced mind:

Balanced Meals: Try to eat a variety of foods. Include plenty of fruits, vegetables, whole grains, and lean proteins. These foods provide the nutrients your brain needs to function well.

Avoid Caffeine and Sugar: Caffeine and sugar can cause spikes in anxiety and make you feel jittery. Instead, opt for water, herbal teas, and natural snacks like nuts and fruits.

Stay Hydrated: Dehydration can affect your mood and energy levels. Make sure you're drinking enough water throughout the day.

Foods that Help Reduce Anxiety

Some foods are particularly good at helping to manage anxiety:

Omega-3 Rich Foods: Foods like salmon, flaxseeds, and walnuts are high in omega-3 fatty acids, which can help reduce anxiety.

Antioxidant-Rich Foods: Berries, spinach, and other colorful fruits and vegetables are full of antioxidants that support brain health.

Probiotics: Yogurt, kefir, and other probiotic-rich foods can improve gut health, which is closely linked to mental health.

The Impact of Regular Exercise

Moving Your Body for a Healthier Mind

Exercise is a powerful tool for managing anxiety. It helps by releasing endorphins, which are natural mood lifters. Here are some ways to get started:

Find What You Enjoy: Whether it's walking, dancing, swimming, or yoga, find an activity that you enjoy. This makes it easier to stick with it.

Start Small: You don't need to run a marathon. Even a short, brisk walk can help reduce anxiety.

Make it Social: Exercising with friends can add an extra layer of support and make the activity more enjoyable.

How Much Exercise is Enough?

Aim for at least 30 minutes of moderate exercise most days of the week. This can be broken down into shorter sessions if that's easier for you. The key is consistency.

Establishing a Healthy Sleep Routine

The Power of Restful Sleep

Good sleep is crucial for managing anxiety. Here's how to improve your sleep habits:

Regular Sleep Schedule: Try to go to bed and wake up at the same time every day, even on weekends. This helps regulate your body's internal clock.

Create a Relaxing Bedtime Routine: Wind down with calming activities like reading, taking a warm bath, or practicing gentle stretches.

Limit Screen Time Before Bed: The blue light from phones and computers can interfere with your sleep. Try to turn off screens at least an hour before bed.

Creating a Sleep-Friendly Environment

Make your bedroom a sanctuary for sleep:

Comfortable Bedding: Invest in a good mattress and pillows.

Dark and Cool Room: A dark, cool environment helps signal to your body that it's time to sleep.

Limit Noise: Use earplugs or a white noise machine if you're in a noisy area.

Creating a Balanced Daily Schedule

Finding Balance in Your Day

A well-balanced schedule can reduce stress and anxiety by providing structure and predictability. Here are some tips:

Prioritize Tasks: Make a list of tasks and prioritize them. Focus on what's most important and try not to overwhelm yourself.

Include Downtime: Schedule time for relaxation and activities that you enjoy. This could be reading, hobbies, or spending time with loved ones.

Break Tasks into Manageable Steps: Large tasks can be intimidating. Break them down into smaller, more manageable steps.

The Importance of Routine

Routines can provide a sense of control and stability, which is particularly helpful when you're feeling anxious. Try to establish daily routines for eating, exercising, and sleeping.

Final Thoughts

32

Making these lifestyle changes can have a profound impact on your anxiety levels. Remember, it's all about taking small, manageable steps and being kind to yourself along the way. You don't have to do everything at once. Start with one change and gradually add others as you feel ready.

Thank you for joining me in this chapter. I hope these tips help you feel more empowered and in control of your anxiety. You deserve to feel your best, and these lifestyle changes can help you get there. If you have any questions or need further support, don't hesitate to reach out.

CHAPTER 6
Building a Support System

Dealing with anxiety can often feel like an overwhelming, solitary journey. However, you don't have to face it alone. Building a strong support system can make a significant difference in managing anxiety. Let's explore how you can create and maintain a network of support that will help you feel understood, connected, and less alone.

The Importance of Social Support

Having people around who care about you can provide comfort and reassurance. Social support helps reduce stress and offers a sense of belonging. When you know that you have someone to talk to, it becomes easier to handle anxious moments.

Why Social Support Matters

Emotional Comfort: Sharing your feelings with someone who listens can provide immediate relief.

Practical Help: Friends and family can offer practical advice and assistance in difficult times.

Perspective: Others can offer a different viewpoint, helping you see situations in a new light.

Communicating Your Needs to Others

It's essential to let people in your life know what you're going through. They can't help if they don't understand your needs. Be honest about your anxiety and what you need from them.

Tips for Effective Communication

Be Honest: Clearly explain what you're experiencing and how it affects you.

Be Specific: Let them know what kind of support you need, whether it's a listening ear, a distraction, or help with tasks.

Be Patient: Understand that not everyone will know how to respond immediately. Give them time to learn and adapt.

Joining Support Groups

Support groups can be a powerful way to connect with others who understand what you're going through. These groups provide a safe space to share experiences and coping strategies.

Benefits of Support Groups

Shared Experiences: Hearing from others who face similar challenges can reduce feelings of isolation.

Mutual Support: Group members can offer and receive support, creating a sense of community.

Learning from Others: You can learn new coping mechanisms and strategies from people who have been in your shoes.

Seeking Professional Help: Therapists and Counselors

Sometimes, professional guidance is necessary to manage anxiety effectively. Therapists and counselors are trained to help you navigate your feelings and develop coping strategies.

Finding the Right Professional

Do Your Research: Look for licensed professionals with experience in treating anxiety.

Ask for Recommendations: Sometimes, a recommendation from a friend or doctor can lead you to the right therapist.

Don't Be Afraid to Switch: If you don't feel comfortable with your therapist, it's okay to find someone else who better fits your needs.

Types of Therapy

Cognitive Behavioral Therapy (CBT): Helps you change negative thought patterns.

Mindfulness-Based Therapy: Focuses on being present and reducing stress through mindfulness techniques.

Exposure Therapy: Gradually exposes you to anxiety-provoking situations to reduce fear.

Building a Support System: A Personal Approach

Creating a support system is a personal journey. It involves recognizing who in your life can provide the emotional and practical support you need and reaching out to them.

Steps to Build Your Support System

1. ***Identify Key People***: Think about friends, family, or colleagues who you trust and feel comfortable with.

2. ***Reach Out***: Don't wait for them to come to you. Take the initiative to contact them.

3. ***Set Boundaries***: Be clear about what you need and what you can give in return. Relationships should be reciprocal.

4. ***Stay Connected:*** Regularly check in with your support network, even when you're feeling okay.

CHAPTER 7
Managing Anxiety in Specific Situations

Anxiety can creep into every part of your life, sometimes unexpectedly. This chapter will help you manage anxiety in various situations, providing practical tips and heartfelt advice to support you when you need it most.

Coping with Anxiety at Work

Understanding Workplace Triggers

Work can be a significant source of stress and anxiety. Deadlines, meetings, and interactions with colleagues can all trigger anxiety. It's essential to identify these triggers to address them effectively.

Creating a Comfortable Workspace

Your workspace can influence your anxiety levels. Try to keep your area tidy and personalize it with things that make you feel calm, like photos or plants. A comfortable chair and good lighting can also make a big difference.

Prioritizing Tasks

When work feels overwhelming, break your tasks into smaller, manageable pieces. Prioritize what needs to be done first and take it one step at a time. Use a to-do list or a planner to keep track of your progress.

Taking Breaks

Don't forget to take regular breaks. Step away from your desk, take a short walk, or do some light stretching. Even a few minutes away from work can help you reset and reduce anxiety.

Communicating with Colleagues

If you're feeling overwhelmed, don't be afraid to talk to a trusted colleague or your manager. They may be able to help lighten your load or offer support. Remember, it's okay to ask for help.

Handling Social Anxiety

Preparing for Social Interactions

Social situations can be daunting if you struggle with social anxiety. Prepare for events by thinking about what you might talk about and practicing conversations. It can also help to arrive early to get comfortable with the environment before it gets busy.

Focusing on Others

Try shifting your focus from yourself to others. Show interest in what they are saying and ask questions. This can help take the pressure off you and make interactions feel more natural.

Using Relaxation Technique

Before and during social events, use relaxation techniques like deep breathing or visualization. Imagine yourself in a calm, happy place to reduce anxiety.

Setting Realistic Goals

Set small, achievable goals for social interactions. It could be something like starting a conversation with one new person or staying at an event for a certain amount of time. Celebrate your successes, no matter how small.

Strategies for Travel Anxiety

Planning Ahead

Travel can be stressful, but planning can help. Make a checklist of everything you need to do and pack. Arrive early to avoid the rush, and familiarize yourself with your itinerary.

Staying Connected

Bring things that comfort you, like a favorite book, music, or a cozy blanket. Staying connected with friends or family through calls or messages can also provide reassurance.

Practicing Mindfulness

Mindfulness can be particularly useful when traveling. Pay attention to your surroundings and try to stay present. Focus on the sights, sounds, and smells around you instead of worrying about what might go wrong.

Being Flexible

Remember that things don't always go as planned. Flights get delayed, plans change, and unexpected issues arise. Try to stay flexible and open-minded, and remind yourself that it's okay if things don't go perfectly.

Managing Health-Related Anxiety

Gathering Information

Health-related anxiety often stems from uncertainty. Educate yourself about your health condition from reliable sources. Understanding your situation can reduce fear of the unknown.

Maintaining a Healthy Lifestyle

Take care of your body with a balanced diet, regular exercise, and enough sleep. These habits can improve your overall well-being and help manage anxiety.

Focusing on What You Can Control

There are aspects of your health that you can control and others that you can't. Focus on what you can do to improve your health, like following your doctor's advice and attending regular check-ups.

Seeking Support

Talk to healthcare professionals about your concerns. They can provide reassurance and practical advice. Support groups or therapy can also be beneficial for dealing with health-related anxiety.

Anxiety can feel isolating, but remember you're not alone. Many people experience anxiety in these situations, and there are strategies and support systems to help you cope. Take it one step at a time, and be kind to yourself as you navigate these challenges.

CHAPTER 8
Long-Term Strategies for Anxiety Management

Developing Resilience

Building resilience is like strengthening your muscles. It takes time and effort, but it pays off in the long run. Resilience helps you bounce back from tough times and keep moving forward. Start by setting small, achievable goals. Celebrate your progress, no matter how small. Remember, every step forward is a victory. Surround yourself with positive influences and don't be afraid to seek help when you need it. You're stronger than you think, and each challenge you overcome makes you even stronger.

Setting Realistic Goals and Expectations

Setting goals can give you direction and purpose, but it's important to be realistic. Break down big goals into smaller, manageable steps. This makes them less overwhelming and more achievable. Be kind to yourself and understand that it's okay to adjust your goals as needed. Life is unpredictable, and flexibility is key. Celebrate your accomplishments, no matter how small, and use them as motivation to keep going. You're doing great, and every step forward is a testament to your strength and determination.

Continuing Your Anxiety Management Journey

Managing anxiety is a journey, not a destination. It's important to keep learning and growing. Stay curious about new techniques and strategies that can help you. Don't be afraid to try different approaches until you find what works best for you. Keep a journal to track your progress and reflect on your experiences. This can help you see how far you've come and identify patterns in your anxiety. Remember, it's okay to have setbacks. They don't erase your progress. Keep moving forward, and know that you're not alone on this journey.

Resources for Ongoing Support and Learning

It's important to have a support system in place as you continue managing your anxiety. Reach out to friends and family who understand and support you. Consider joining a support group, either in person or online. There are many resources available that can provide guidance and encouragement. Look for books, podcasts, and websites dedicated to anxiety management. Consider seeking professional help from a therapist or counselor. They can provide valuable insights and tools to help you on your journey. Remember, seeking help is a sign of strength, not weakness. You're taking control of your well-being, and that's something to be proud of.

Developing Resilience

Building resilience is a bit like getting fit—it takes time, effort, and persistence, but the results are worth it. Think of resilience as your ability to bounce back from life's challenges. Every time you face a tough situation and come through it, you get a little stronger.

Start by setting small goals for yourself. They don't have to be big; even small achievements can make a huge difference. Celebrate these victories, no matter how minor they seem. Each one is a step forward.

Surround yourself with positive people who lift you up. It's okay to ask for help when you need it. Remember, you're stronger than you realize. Each challenge you overcome is a testament to your resilience.

Setting Realistic Goals and Expectations

Goals give you direction and something to strive for, but it's crucial to set realistic ones. Break big goals into smaller, manageable steps. This way, they seem less daunting and more achievable.

Be kind to yourself. It's perfectly okay to adjust your goals as you go along. Life is full of surprises, and flexibility is important. Celebrate your achievements, no matter how small they are. Every small win is a step in the right direction.

You're making progress every day, and that's something to be proud of. Keep going, and remember that you're doing great.

Continuing Your Anxiety Management Journey

Managing anxiety is an ongoing process. It's not about reaching a final destination but about continuously learning and adapting. Stay open to new techniques and strategies. What works today might not work tomorrow, and that's okay.

Keep a journal of your progress. Write down what works and what doesn't. Reflecting on your experiences can help you understand your anxiety better and see how far you've come.

Setbacks are a part of the journey. They don't mean you're failing; they're just a bump in the road. Keep moving forward, and remember, you're not alone.

Resources for Ongoing Support and Learning

Having a support system is essential. Reach out to friends and family who understand what you're going through. Join support groups, either in person or online, where you can share experiences and gain encouragement.

Explore books, podcasts, and websites dedicated to anxiety management. There's a wealth of information out there. Don't hesitate to seek professional help from therapists or counselors. They can offer valuable tools and insights.

Remember, asking for help is a sign of strength. You're taking charge of your mental health, and that's something to be proud of.

I hope this chapter helps you understand that managing anxiety is a journey, not a destination. Each step you take is progress, and you should be proud of yourself for making the effort. Keep going, stay positive, and remember that you're stronger than you think.

CONCLUSION

As you reach the end of this journey on managing anxiety, take a moment to acknowledge your courage and determination. Dealing with anxiety is not an easy path, but every step you've taken toward understanding and managing it is a testament to your strength and resilience.

Remember, managing anxiety is an ongoing process. It's about making small, consistent efforts every day. Celebrate your progress, no matter how minor it may seem. Each step forward is a victory, and every setback is an opportunity to learn and grow.

You are not alone. There are countless resources and people who understand what you're going through. Lean on your support system, seek out new strategies, and never hesitate to ask for help when you need it. Your journey is unique, but you share it with many others who are also striving to manage their anxiety.

Most importantly, be kind to yourself. Practice self-compassion and recognize that it's okay to have tough days. Your worth is not defined by your anxiety, but by your perseverance and the love you give to yourself and others.

Keep moving forward with hope and confidence. You have the tools and the strength within you to create a life filled with peace and fulfillment. Your journey is just beginning, and the best is yet to come.